From Renting to Owning
A Journey to Financial Autonomy

Table of Contents

Chapter 1. Introduction

In our latest Special Report: "From Renting to Owning: A Journey to Financial Autonomy", we excitedly explore the empowering process of transitioning from a renter to a homeowner. An important step towards financial independence, this shift is more than just a change in living arrangements - it is a life-changing decision teeming with potential benefits. We confidently guide you through each phase of this journey, taking care to provide valuable insights, practical advice, and motivating stories of those who've successfully navigated these waters before. Whether you're at the start of your journey or considering this major leap, this report is a cheerfully supportive and all-encompassing guide filled with indispensable nuggets of wisdom. Packed full of optimism, practicality, and financial savvy, this report is your indispensable companion on your remarkable journey towards owning your dream home and achieving financial autonomy.

Chapter 2. Understanding the Basics: What it Means to Own Your Home

Owning a home is more than just possessing a physical structure where you live; it's an embodiment of personal freedom and a significant step towards financial independence. Yet, comprehending what homeownership truly signifies requires an understanding of several interconnected elements. This chapter aims to unravel these intrinsic details surrounding homeownership and guide aspiring homeowners towards this gratifying achievement.

2.1. The Concept of Homeownership

Homeownership offers the control and stability that renting can never provide. It's about having a place that you can call your own, where you can express your individuality by tailoring the space according to your taste without needing the landlord's approval. Homeownership essentially gives you a solid foundation, both literally and figuratively, to build your life.

But homeownership is not merely about expressive freedom or stability; it's a financial commitment. Owning a home means being responsible for mortgage payments, home maintenance, and property tax, among other things. Similarly, homeownership can also be seen as an investment; as property values typically rise over time, the owner stands a chance to secure a valuable asset.

2.2. Advantages and Challenges of Homeownership

When delving deeper into what it means to own a home, one must consider both the advantages and potential challenges.

From the aspect of advantages, the most prominent one is building equity. As you pay off your mortgage, your ownership stake or 'equity' in your home grows. Equity is a powerful thing - you can use it for home improvements, pay off debts, or even plan for retirement.

Plus, let's not forget the sense of stability homeownership can offer. Your home is your haven, safe from hikes in rent, or eviction at the landlord's whim.

On the flip side, one significant challenge of owning is that it's a hefty financial responsibility that involves different types of costs, from mortgage payments to unexpected repairs.

Let's further break down the advantages and challenges into perceivable sections.

Advantages	Challenges
Building Equity	Mortgage payments
Stability	Unexpected repairs
Freedom and Personalization	Property taxes, insurance
Tax Benefits	Home maintenance
Potential for Rental Income	Limited mobility

2.3. Understanding Homeownership Costs

To fully comprehend homeownership, let's dive into what these costs typically are:

- Mortgage payments: This is the money you borrow to pay for your home. The amount of your mortgage depends on the price of the home minus your down payment.

- Home insurance: Insurance that covers the structure of your home and your belongings from damage.

- Property taxes: Local governments impose taxes based on the assessed value of your home.

- Maintenance & repairs: Cost for routine maintenance and unexpected repairs that your home may need over time.

- Utilities: You will be responsible for paying all utilities including electricity, water, sewage, and possibly others like gas and garbage disposal.

The accompanying table gives a comparative insight into the homeownership costs versus renting.

Renter	Homeowner
Rental payments	Mortgage payments
Renter's insurance (less expensive)	Homeowner's insurance
Possibly some utilities	All utilities
Possible renters tax credits	Property taxes
No repair costs (generally)	Maintenance and repair costs

2.4. From Renting to Owning: The Transition

The transition from being a renter to a homeowner can be a daunting one. While as a renter, you are generally not responsible for maintenance or repair costs, as a homeowner, these fall squarely on your shoulders. You also have to take into account other costs like property taxes, homeowner's insurance, and possibly homeowner's association fees.

But on the upside, being a homeowner means building equity. Each mortgage payment you make helps build your financial stake in your home. And over time, if property values increase, those gains are yours to keep. In contrast, when renting, your money goes to the landlord and you aren't building any equity.

2.5. The Emotional Aspect of Homeownership

Owning a home can bring immense emotional satisfaction. It can offer a sense of security, belonging, and permanence. The pride of homeownership can bestow a level of comfort and essence of achievement like no other.

But alongside the joy, there could be added stress too. The responsibility of maintenance, the financial commitment, and the worry of property value may sometimes cause anxiety.

Our journey towards understanding homeownership may stir up complex emotions, and here we can see a few:

Joy and Pride   Stress and Anxiety

| Sense of Permanence | Responsibility and Commitment |
| Belongingness | Worry about Property Value |

Understanding homeownership means understanding these multiple facets. And as we journey towards it, it becomes a perfect blend of financial, emotional, and practical factors that synergizes what a 'home' truly represents. As we embrace homeownership, we don't just acquire a property; we are gradually stepping into a new lifestyle filled with its unique experiences and prospects. This move towards financial autonomy is indeed a significant milestone in our journey of life.

Chapter 3. Decoding Financial Autonomy: An Intuitive Guide

Financial autonomy - a term that sounds daunting, but which is inherently liberating. Essentially, it refers to the ability to be in full control of your financial destiny. Achieving financial autonomy is a crucial milestone in our transition from renting to owning, and this journey, while uniquely subjective, has a few common key aspects we will explore together in this insightful guide.

3.1. The Foundations of Financial Autonomy

The road to financial autonomy is paved with discipline, strategy, and knowledge. First, it is essential to understand that financial autonomy is not just about money. Yes, wealth plays an integral role, but the true essence of financial autonomy lies in effectively managing resources to achieve your life's objectives.

Chapter 4. Understanding Your Financial Status

The first step is to gauge where you currently stand financially. Start by listing down your assets and liabilities. The difference between the two is your net worth.

> * Listing your assets: These include tangible items like cars, houses, and cash, or intangible ones such as investments and savings. Estimate their current market value.
> * Listing your liabilities: These include any debts or responsibilities you need to cover.
> * Calculate your net worth: Subtract your liabilities from your assets.

Having a clear picture of your financial standing allows you to strategize and set realistic goals towards achieving financial autonomy.

4.1. Establishing Your Financial Goals

Financial autonomy cannot be achieved without a clear definition of your financial goals. Remember, your financial goals should be SMART – Specific, Measurable, Achievable, Relevant, and Time-bound. Here's a practical example of a SMART goal: "I want to save $100,000 for a house down payment in 5 years."

Chapter 5. Drafting a Concrete Financial Plan

Equipped with a clear understanding of your financial status and established financial goals, you are ready to design a financial plan. This plan should outline how you intend to spend, save, and invest to accumulate the necessary wealth.

A typical financial plan might encompass:

```
* Revenue stream: Detail your income sources and look
for ways to increase them.
* Expenditure: Categorize your spending into essential
and non-essential expenses.
* Saving: Start with small amounts and gradually
increase as you stabilize your spending.
* Investing: Consider different opportunities like
stocks, bonds, mutual funds, and real estate, among
others.
* Risk Management: Evaluate possible risks and how to
mitigate them.
```

Remember to revise your plan periodically to accommodate lifestyle changes and fluctuations in market conditions.

5.1. Building an Emergency Fund

Your financial plan should also include building an emergency fund. This fund acts as a safety net in case of unexpected expenses or difficulties. A good starting point may be to allocate a part of your income into a high-interest savings account.

5.2. Understanding and Utilizing Credit

A responsible approach to credit is crucial on your journey to financial autonomy. By making timely repayments and minimizing credit use, you can build your credit score, and this can help you secure better mortgage rates when buying your desired home.

5.3. Investing Towards Your Future

Investing is a powerful way to grow wealth over time. Regularly investing a part of your income into different portfolios can help you massively scale up your financial resources. However, take time to understand the risk levels of your investments and align them with your financial goals.

5.4. Continuous Learning and Adapting

Financial autonomy requires being adaptable and consistently learning about new financial strategies and opportunities. Subscribe to financial publications, join finance-related webinars, or even get a coach.

5.5. Financial Autonomy and Homeownership

Your journey to financial autonomy will come full circle when you accomplish your dream of homeownership. Converting the monthly rental costs into mortgage repayments allows you to build equity in your property, an asset you can use to further your financial independence.

Remember, financial autonomy is not a one-size-fits-all model; the journey is subjective and is best charted by each person's unique life situation and objectives. With time, discipline, and strategic planning, your transition from a renter to a homeowner while achieving financial autonomy is possible.

Chapter 6. Renting vs Owning: A Comparative Analysis

Opening the door to homeownership requires a clear understanding of the differences between renting and owning. This lays down the groundwork, helping you make informed decisions that will solely determine the trajectory of your journey towards attaining financial independence.

Before embarking on your pathway to homeownership, it's highly fundamental to digest the benefits and drawbacks of both renting and owning — this is undoubtedly one of the most integral parts of realizing your dream of owning your home.

6.1. Renting: The Basics

Renting a home typically involves entering into a contract with a landlord or property manager. For some, this might be the right move. Renting has many advantages, although it also comes with a share of drawbacks.

Table 1. Ascertain Aspects of Renting

Pros	Cons
Flexibility	Renters can move easily after their lease expires, making this a smart option for those who anticipate changing jobs or for those who simply enjoy switching scenery every few years.

Pros	Cons
No Equity	The key disadvantage to renting is that you're essentially paying someone else's mortgage without gaining any equity in return. Over time, this may lead to a feeling of lost investment.
No Maintenance Costs	Renters are generally not responsible for home repairs or maintenance, which can lead to savings over time.
No Control Over Rent Increases	Rent can be increased at the end of each lease term. There's also no guarantee that a lease will be renewed.
Potentially Lower Cost	Renting might be cheaper in the short term because it does not include expenses such as home repairs and property taxes.
Limited Ability to Customize	Renters are usually not allowed to make significant alterations to their rentals without permission from the landlord.

6.2. Homeownership: What it Entails

Homeownership signifies more than just having your name on a deed — it's about planting roots, becoming part of a community, and, most importantly, gaining financial independence. Similar to renting, homeownership also has clear pros and cons.

Table 2. Ascertain Aspects of Homeownership

Pros	Cons
Building Equity	Unlike renters, homeowners gradually pay off their mortgages and increase their equity in the property.

Pros	Cons
Higher Up-Front Costs	Downpayments, closing costs, and other expenses can make buying a house more costly than renting.
Freedom to Customize	You have the freedom to remodel, redecorate, and change your home however you want.
Maintenance and Repairs	On the flip side, as a homeowner, you are responsible for all costs related to maintaining and repairing your home, which can add up over time.
Possible Tax Benefits	Homeowners may be eligible for certain tax benefits, possibly reducing the net cost of homeownership.
Potential for Financial Loss	While a home may increase in value over time, there's always the risk of a decrease in the market. Homeowners might end up owing more than their home is worth.

6.3. Making the Comparative Leap

After understanding the individual facets of both renting and owning, the next significant stride involves comparing these factors side by side. This involves examining potential financial responsibilities, lifestyle implications, and long-term impacts.

6.4. The Financial Angle

One pivotal contrast revolves around the financial implications of renting versus buying. For many, owning a home represents a sound long-term investment, but it's also a decision that comes with upfront costs.

For renters, costs might be lower initially, and it might feel like you have more financial flexibility on a month-to-month basis. However, you also miss out on the potential long-term economic benefits of homeownership such as equity buildup and possible tax advantages.

6.5. The Lifestyle Perspective

Another key component lies in how each option fits your lifestyle. Buying a home offers a sense of permanence and the ability to personalize your space freely. However, it does mean more responsibilities and commitments.

Renting can be a better option for those who prefer fewer responsibilities, enjoy changing their living environment frequently, or those who need to travel extensively for work — it offers a degree of flexibility that owning does not.

6.6. Taking the Long View

Homeownership can offer financial stability in the long run, building equity, setting a fixed cost for housing (assuming a fixed-rate mortgage), and potentially providing a sizeable payout if you decide to sell.

Renting might bring a measure of flexibility and freedom, albeit without establishing any long-term wealth or stability — a significant piece of the puzzle when considering future financial health.

6.7. Conclusion: An Individual Journey

Ultimately, the choice between renting and owning is a highly personal decision. It depends upon factors such as financial readiness, lifestyle preferences, long-term goals, and market conditions. The journey from renting to homeownership is an empowering process and an instrumental step towards financial independence.

This chapter aimed to deliver a detailed comparative analysis to assist you in making an informed decision, facilitating your journey towards financial autonomy. Digging into the subsequent chapters of this report will further equip you in embarking on this exciting path.

No hard and fast rule exists when it comes to choosing between renting and buying. In the end, the best choice is the one that aligns with your personal goals, realities, and aspirations and leads you towards your envisioned future of financial freedom.

Chapter 7. Prerequisites to Home Ownership: Preparing for the Big Leap

Becoming a homeowner is a thrilling prospect, but it also requires thorough planning and preparation. A successful transition requires concerted effort on multiple fronts: financial, legal, and lifestyle-related. To best prepare yourself, you need a strong foundation of knowledge and an understanding of what to expect along the way.

7.1. Financial Readiness

Understanding your financial status is the linchpin that holds the process of transitioning to homeownership together. Before thinking of owning a home, consider the following financial aspects.

7.1.1. Current Savings

Your savings will mainly be used for the down payment, closing costs and any unexpected costs that might arise throughout the process. Experts recommend having at least 20% of the home's price for the down payment, although some loans offer lower down payment options. As a rough guideline, aside from the down payment, ensure you have enough savings to cover 2–4% of the home's purchase price for closing costs.

7.1.2. Monthly Income and Expenditures

Analyzing monthly income against your expenditures will help you assess if you can afford a mortgage, which is typically the most significant monthly expense for homeowners. A useful rule of thumb is the 28% rule, which suggests that your housing expenses (mortgage payment, insurance, property taxes) should not exceed 28% of your gross monthly income.

7.1.3. Credit Score

Your credit score impacts the interest rates offered on your mortgage. It can be advantageous to review your credit score well in advance and correct any mistakes or work on improving it if necessary.

7.1.4. Debt-to-Income Ratio

Lenders generally favor a debt-to-income (DTI) ratio of 36% or lower, including your future mortgage payments. Calculate your current DTI and work on reducing it if it is high.

7.2. Understanding the Housing Market

Market fluency can affect your successful transition to homeownership. A good understanding of the housing market at both national and local levels is instrumental in timing your purchase well. Know the average property prices, demand and supply trends, projected price changes to make informed decisions.

7.3. Choosing the Ideal Location

The location of your home significantly affects its price, livability, and potential resale value. Consider factors like proximity to workplaces, schools, healthcare, and leisure facilities according to your needs. Ensure you research the neighborhood's safety, future community development plans, property taxes, and average utility costs.

7.4. Long-Term Commitment

Owning a home goes beyond its financial implications—it indeed is a long-term commitment. Evaluating your needs, life goals, and mobility can help determine if you are ready for it.

7.5. Pre-Qualification and Pre-Approval

Lastly, securing pre-qualification and pre-approval from lenders provides an idea of what you can afford, making the home shopping process smoother. The difference between the two is that pre-approval is a more in-depth verification process, providing a specific loan amount.

7.6. Partnering With a Real Estate Agent

Developing a working relationship with a real estate agent helps streamline the process. Their knowledge, expertise, and networks can save time and effort, and often, they can negotiate better deals on your behalf.

The road to homeownership is a challenging yet fulfilling one. With careful preparation, you can navigate this path with confidence and move a step closer to your dream home and financial independence. Remember, every small step towards homeownership is a significant leap towards financial autonomy.

Chapter 8. The Economics of Ownership: The Durable Investment

As you embark on the journey of home ownership, understanding the economics of this venture is crucial. It's not merely about having a roof over your head, but more importantly, it's about making a durable investment that can benefit you significantly in the long run.

8.1. Understanding the Concept of Home Ownership as an Investment

Before delving deeper, it's important to conceptualize home ownership as an investment. When you buy a home, you're investing in a tangible asset that has the potential to appreciate over time. This is unlike rent payments, which offer no return and can even increase unpredictably over time.

When you own a home, you have full control over your living space. This means you can make improvements and renovations that could boost your home's market value. Additionally, you slowly build equity as you continue making mortgage payments and gradually own more of the property outright.

8.2. The Relationship Between Housing Market and Economy

Most economic indicators affect the real estate market, making it vital to understand their interplay. Essentially, when the economy is thriving, both the demand for homes and home prices increase. Conversely, during economic downturns, home prices may stagnitate or decrease, but it's important to note that over the past half-century, the overall trend for home prices in the United States has been an upward one.

It's also important to understand how interest rates influence the housing market. When interest rates are low, borrowing money to buy a home becomes less expensive, which encourages people to buy. As demand increases, so do prices.

8.3. Equity Building: A Form of Saving

One advantageous aspect of home ownership is the opportunity for equity building, which can be seen as a form of automatic saving. Every time you make a mortgage payment, a portion of that payment goes towards the principal on your loan, which increases your equity, or your ownership stake in your home.

Over time, as you pay down the principal on your mortgage, the equity you've built can be substantial. This can provide you with a significant financial resource. You may be able to borrow against your equity to fund home improvements, pay down debt, or cover other large expenses.

8.4. Tax Advantages of Home Ownership

Another critical economic factor is the possible tax benefits that come with home ownership. These benefits vary depending on the region, but a common advantage is the ability to deduct mortgage interest and property tax payments from your taxable income. This can potentially result in substantial tax savings.

Remember, it's critical to consult with a tax professional to understand the tax implications and benefits applicable to your specific situation before making a decision.

8.5. Preparing for the Costs of Home Ownership

Though home ownership comes with numerous financial benefits, it's important not to overlook the myriad costs associated with owning and maintaining a home. These expenses include, but are not limited to, mortgage payments, property taxes, home insurance, and repair and maintenance costs. It is important to factor these into your budget when considering the affordability of a home.

8.6. Investing for the Future: Generational Wealth

Owning a home is often seen as an essential step in building generational wealth, as homes can be passed down from generation to generation. This asset accumulation across generations can lead to significant financial stability and prosperity for future members of your family.

In conclusion, transitioning from renting to home ownership is a substantial and empowering step offering potential financial benefits in the form of equity building, potential tax advantages, and future wealth generation. While home ownership does come with costs and responsibilities, understanding the economics of this venture can help you minimize risks and maximize gains, facilitating your journey towards financial autonomy.

Chapter 9. Assessing Your Readiness: A Self-Evaluation Toolkit

Before embarking on the exciting journey towards homeownership, it's crucial to evaluate your readiness. This will help create a stronger foundation, making the transition smoother. Assessing your readiness takes into consideration multiple facets such as financial health, creditworthiness, lifestyle compatibility, and emotional preparedness. In the following sections, we delve into the specifics of each aspect.

9.1. Understanding Your Financial Health

The initial step to assess readiness for homeownership revolves around gauging financial health. This is not only about your present financial state but also about the stability of your income and future growth potential. Consider the following points:

Current Savings: Your current savings are critical to cover upfront costs such as down payment, closing fees, and moving costs. A helpful equation could be the following: $$ \text{Current Savings} - (\text{Down Payment} + \text{Closing Fees} + \text{Moving Costs}) $$ If the result is negative or close to zero, it might be an indicator that you need to postpone homeownership until you've built up more savings.

Future Savings: Besides your current savings, projecting your future savings based on your current income and expenses is necessary. This can help you understand if you will be able to continue saving or even sustain your lifestyle after investing in a property.

A Stable Source of Income: It's essential to have a stable source of income to manage the monthly mortgage payments, maintenance costs, and unforeseen expenses related to homeownership. Ensure that your job or business is secure, and you have options if things change unexpectedly.

Debt-to-income (DTI) Ratio: A critical aspect that lenders look at is your DTI ratio - the percentage of your gross income that goes towards repaying debts. Make sure your DTI ratio (including your proposed mortgage payments) stays below the typically recommended ratio of 36%.

9.2. Checking Your Creditworthiness

Your credit score directly influences the interest rate on your mortgage – the higher your score, the lower your interest rate. Before deciding to buy a house, check your credit score and credit history.

Credit Score: Knowing your credit score can help you know if your application for a loan would likely be approved, and what sort of interest rate you can expect.

Credit History: Lenders also look at your credit history to see if you've been reliable with past repayments. You'll need a satisfactory credit history to qualify for the most favorable loan terms.

If your credit score or credit history seems unsatisfactory, it might be better to delay your plans until your credit health improves.

9.3. Ensuring Lifestyle Compatibility

Homeownership is as much about finances as it is about lifestyle. Remember, a home is a long-term commitment – emotionally, financially, and geographically.

Geographical Stability: If your lifestyle or job requires you to move around often, renting might be a better option.

Spatial Needs: Buying a larger home than necessary will only add to your mortgage and maintenance cost. Consider your requirement in terms of space effectively.

Personal Readiness: Owning a home comes with its set of responsibilities like maintenance and repair that were previously taken care of by the landlord when renting. You should be prepared to handle such responsibilities.

9.4. Emotional Preparedness

Lastly, ensure that you are emotionally ready for homeownership.

Market Fluctuations: Be prepared for possible changes in property value due to market fluctuations.

Calculating Risks: It's essential to consider the worst-case scenarios – a significant drop in property value, an unexpected job loss, or an unforeseen expense.

Satisfaction and Achievement: Remember, homeownership is part of the American Dream for a reason. Despite the challenges, owning a home can bring immense satisfaction, security, and a sense of achievement.

In summary, transitioning from renting to owning is a journey filled with challenges and rewards. By evaluating your readiness across these important parameters, you can better prepare for the road to homeownership.

Chapter 10. Kicking off the Home-Buying Journey: Tips and Strategies

Stepping into the world of real estate as a potential homeowner can be thrilling, yet overwhelming at first. The possession of your own dwelling isn't just about having a roof over your head. It symbolizes autonomy, maturity, and accomplishment. However, the journey to homeownership requires preparation, strategy, and a lot of research. Here are some of our best tips and strategies for you to kick off your home-buying journey.

10.1. The Home-Buying Mindset

So, you have decided to buy your first home. Excellent! The initial step in this process isn't finding the right realtor or even figuring out your budget. It's about becoming a successful home buyer, which starts with your mindset. Understand that the home-buying process is often complex and unpredictable. Embrace this reality and prepare yourself to handle the challenges that may arise. Keep in mind your ultimate goal: transitioning from renter to homeowner.

10.2. Understand your Finances

Understanding your financial situation is a crucial early step of your home-buying journey. Analyze your cash flow to determine how much you can realistically afford. Remember that homeowner costs include not only mortgage payments, but also property tax, homeowner's insurance, and maintenance.

To determine your potential mortgage payment, you can make use of online mortgage calculators. Factor in your current debt payments, like student loans, credit card bills, and car payments, as these will impact the amount of mortgage you can afford.

Also, maintain a solid emergency fund. This foresight will give you the financial confidence and preparatory skills needed for homeownership.

10.3. Find out your Credit Score

Before contacting banks for a loan, review your credit report. A high credit score can get you a better interest rate on your loan, saving a significant amount of money over time. If your credit score is not up to the mark, try to improve it by paying bills on time, reducing outstanding debts, and avoiding new debts.

10.4. Choosing the right Mortgage

Different mortgages offer different rates, and it's essential to choose the one best tailored to your financial situation. Research on fixed-rate vs. adjustable-rate mortgages, think about loan terms, and to what extent you're ready to put cash down to decide what's best for you. Our suggestion is always to consult with a mortgage professional to gain an accurate understanding.

10.5. Defining your Ideal Home

Identify your must-haves, your nice-to-haves, and your cannot-haves in your future home. This list will not only streamline your hunt for your dream home but also help prevent you from impulse buying a property that fails to meet your needs.

10.6. Locating a Good Realtor

Working with a good realtor can drastically simplify your home-buying process. They can guide you about the local housing market, help negotiate your offers, and lead you through piles of paperwork. Moreover, your realtor should have a wealth of experience, an understanding of your needs and concerns, and the ability to act in your best interest.

10.7. Making the Offer

Once you've found the ideal home, it's time to make an offer. Your realtor will guide you on the price to offer, any conditions you should include, and what the timeline should be.

Also, be prepared for negotiations. You may have to raise your offer price or waive certain continganices to close the deal depending upon the seller's response.

10.8. Getting a Home Inspection

After your offer has been accepted, it's highly recommended to have a professional home inspection. An inspection can reveal hidden issues with the property, giving you a chance to negotiate repairs with the seller, or in some cases, walk away from the transaction.

Embarking on your home buying journey is a significant step towards establishing your own financial independence. It's a process, and like any process, it can seem daunting at times. However, with the right mindset, thorough planning, due diligence, and expert guidance, you can navigate the complexities efficiently. The end result? Your dream home, and the prized experience of being a homeowner. Make every step count, and be excited about what's ahead!

Chapter 11. Overcoming the Hurdles: Learning from Successful Homeowners' Experiences

Transitioning from renting to owning is certainly a rewarding yet challenging journey. Every prospective homeowner faces hurdles, and learning to overcome these obstacles is key to successfully owning a home. To guide you through this process, we've gathered invaluable experience from successful homeowners.

11.1. Understanding the Financial Implications

Buying a home is a significant financial commitment, and understanding the financial implications is crucial. Successful homeowners make it a point to thoroughly comprehend their financial situation before embarking on the homeownership journey.

To begin, take a careful look at your current financial situation. It's essential to understand your cash flow – income and expenditure – and the surplus, if any, at the end of each month. Factor in all your routine expenses, including transportation, utilities, groceries, and any outstanding loans or credit card dues. It is critical to assess if you will still have comfortable leftover income after managing the expected monthly home loan repayments.

It's also important to understand the various costs involved in buying a home, starting from the down payment, which typically falls between 10-20% of the property's price, to closing costs, moving expenses, and the cost of life after moving in – including maintenance and utility costs.

As you explore mortgages, take note of the interest rates, term, and monthly payments. Compare these details among different lenders to ensure you get the best deal. Remember, the lowest interest rate might not always be the best choice if it comes with high fees or unfavorable terms.

11.2. Saving for the Down Payment

Once you've understood the financial implications of buying a home, the next step is collecting the down payment. This is often one of the most significant hurdles prospective homeowners face. However, successful homeowners often share that with patience, discipline, and the right saving strategies, this hurdle can be easily overcome.

Start by setting a realistic saving goal for your down payment. This target should be based on the price range of homes you are considering and your current financial situation.

Next, review your monthly expense and identify areas where you can cut back. It could be anything from dining out less to choosing a more affordable car. Remember, each dollar saved is a dollar earned towards your dream home.

Consider opening a separate savings account for your home's down payment. This helps in tracking your progress and reduces the temptation to dip into these funds for other expenses.

11.3. The Importance of a Good Credit Score

A good credit score is a vital part of the puzzle in the home buying process. It influences your borrowing cost and whether you even qualify for a mortgage. Successful homeowners work diligently to maintain or improve their credit score.

Start by getting a copy of your credit report and thoroughly reviewing it. Correct any inaccuracies as these could negatively impact your credit score. Pay particular attention to your debt and ensure timely payments.

Reducing your credit card balance can also have a positive effect on your credit score. A good thumb rule is to keep the utilized credit under 30% of your total credit limit. Remember, building or improving a credit score takes time, so start as early as possible in your homeownership journey.

11.4. Deciding on Your Dream Home

Deciding on your dream home's specifications can be both exciting and challenging. It involves striking a balance between wants and needs, short-term benefits, and long-term value.

Successful homeowners insist on staying grounded to their financial reality while imagining their dream home. Rather than being carried away by the luxury, focus on what matters most - affordability, the location's comfort and convenience, and the home size.

Your dream home should be within your budget, in a location that saves your commuting time, large enough for your current or planned family size, and, of course, should be a place where you feel at home.

11.5. Navigating the Real Estate Jargons and Procedures

Navigating the real estate world can be confusing, with its myriad of jargons and procedures. Breaking down the complex terms and understanding standard home-buying procedures is the key.

Start by familiarizing yourself with common real estate terms, such as escrow, pre-approval, fixed-rate mortgage, adjustable-rate mortgage and so on. While real estate agents or brokers can guide you, understanding these terms enhances your grasp of the process.

Learn about the standard home-buying procedures in your country or state. This knowledge will provide a sense of control during the home buying process.

11.6. Embracing the Unpredictability

Finally, it's important to accept the unpredictability of the property market. Successful homeowners have reiterated that patience, resilience, and flexibility played an essential role in their journey.

Random maintenance issues, unexpected market fluctuations, changes in interest rates, or shifts in personal circumstances are uncertainties inherent in this journey. Embrace this unpredictability, adapt and adjust your plans as needed, and remember - each hurdle crossed gets you one step closer to your dream home.

After all, the transition from renting to owning is not just about financial independence. It's about building a nest that embodies your personality, a place where you can make beautiful memories with family and friends.

These insights from successful homeowners can shape your understanding, preparation, and execution of your homeownership strategy. Armed with this knowledge and backed by your hard work, you are now well equipped to face any hurdles on your journey to becoming a homeowner — Here's to your successful home ownership!

Chapter 12. Securing Your Investment: Ensuring Long-Term Success

The decision to transition from renting to owning is undeniably a significant one. But once the decision is made, another vital task is laid out before you: securing your investment. Investing in a house can be a great financial move, but without the correct strategies, it can also lead to financial pitfalls.

Transforming from a renter to a homeowner is a journey, not an overnight switch. It takes time, patience, and insightful planning. Furthermore, long-term success in homeownership isn't just about meeting mortgage repayments. It's about understanding the broader financial landscape surrounding your new asset, putting up a defense against potential risks, and ensuring the value of your home appreciates over time.

Let's dive into the comprehensive steps that will help you protect your investment for long-term success.

12.1. Understanding the Housing Market

Understanding the housing market is crucial. That's why, before purchasing a property, it's vital to research the historical trends of your desired location. Look at the property value trends in your area, paying attention to the pace of growth. Slow, steady growth could imply a stable investment.

Anticipate fluctuations in the market and consider how they might impact your property's value. Remember, housing demand is influenced by various factors like population growth, employment opportunities, and developments in infrastructure, all of which can fluctuate. Take note of these factors in your location of interest.

Despite all your research, remember that predicting the real estate market is a complex task - even professionals don't always get it right. So, keep an eye on the broader economic indicators, make educated estimates, and remain prepared for some level of uncertainty.

12.2. Maintenance and Upkeep

The cost of maintaining a home can be significantly higher than that of a rental. As a renter, issues like a leaky roof or a broken AC might mean a call to your landlord. But as a homeowner, these costs fall on you.

So, part of ensuring your investment's long-term success is setting up an emergency fund. As a general rule of thumb, earmark 1-2% of your home's value per year for maintenance and repairs. This fund should be over and above your regular savings or emergency fund as it's specifically for home-related costs.

Remember, maintenance isn't just about preventing problems or fixing them as they occur. Regular maintenance can also add to your home value. Renovations like updating the kitchen or bathroom, or landscaping upgrades can increase attractiveness and thereby the market value of your home.

12.3. Home Insurance

Shielding your investment from any unforeseen damage is essential. This is where home insurance comes into play. Choose a home insurance policy that covers your property but also any valuable possessions inside your home.

The cost of insurance can be impacted by factors such as the location of your property, the size of your home, and even things like the proximity of your home to a fire station. It's good to set time aside to research and understand these influencing factors so you can find a policy that fits your needs best without breaking your budget.

12.4. Diversifying Your Investment

Securing your investment also pertains to the principle of not putting all your eggs in one basket.

While it's true that homeownership is a significant investment, it shouldn't be your only one. Diversify by investing in different asset classes such as stocks, bonds, mutual funds, and even retirement accounts. The goal is to mitigate risks and maximize returns.

12.5. Building Equity

Building equity - the part of the property you truly own - is a journey of its own. With each mortgage payment, you're increasing your equity, reducing what you owe to the lender. Importantly, if the value of your home increases over time, your equity can grow without you even realizing it.

To expedite this, consider making larger or more frequent payments, but ensure your budget can handle it comfortably. If your financial situation allows, you can also opt to refinance your loan for a shorter term. However, always take time to gauge the potential benefits against any associated costs or penalties.

12.6. Conclusion

Securing your investment is about understanding the dynamics of the housing market, being prepared for the costs that come with homeownership, and making strategic decisions about insurance, diversification, and equity building.

It's crucial to acknowledge this process as an ongoing one, just like the journey from renter to homeowner. It requires patience and plenty of active learning. However, with careful planning and deliberate action, you have the power to safeguard your investment and strive towards a future of financial autonomy.

Chapter 13. Celebrating Success: Enjoying Your Journey to Financial Autonomy

Your journey from being a renter to a homeowner is a strenuous process, albeit one filled with numerous accomplishments that should be celebrated. Each step you take brings you closer to the financial autonomy you seek. Along this journey, there are milestones and victories, large and small, that should be recognized and celebrated. These victories not only symbolize progress but also motivate us to keep going and reach our ultimate goal.

13.1. Acknowledging Progress and Milestones

Let's begin by identifying what these milestones might be. They could range from saving for your first down payment to paying off that first mortgage payment. Each of these achievements, no matter how small, are steps that carry you closer to your financial independence.

To celebrate these victories, you first need to acknowledge them. Keep a record of where you started and what you have achieved. This way, you can visually see what you have done so far. Having a physical or digital journal of your progress can be incredibly motivating. You could use asciidoc tables to keep your record organized.

```
[cols="2,2,5",options="header"]
|===
```

```
| Milestone | Date | Notes
| Saved 10% for down payment | June 4, 2022 | Came from
setting aside 20% of each paycheck and cutting back on
dining out.
| Paid off first mortgage payment | July 1, 2022 | Great
feeling! Looking forward to more successful payments.
|===
```

13.2. Tools to Track Progress

To track your progress with us today, there are several digital tools that can help. Some apps track your financial goals in real-time, offer advice, and even give you a virtual pat on the back when you achieve a target. Choose the tool that fits your needs, and start celebrating your achievements today.

Remember, success is a journey, not a destination. It doesn't end with one goal, but continues with the next. This mindset is especially applicable as you strive towards financial autonomy. You don't just stop at buying your first house. You keep going, perhaps investing in another property or starting a retirement fund.

13.3. Celebrating Financial Successes

What's progress without a bit of celebration? Once you reach a financial milestone, it's crucial to celebrate. Whether that celebration is a quiet dinner at home, a night out, or a small gift to yourself, make it something enjoyable. Celebrating your successes, no matter how small, will not only help keep up your morale but also spur you on to your next financial goal.

13.4. Rewarding Your Grit and Perseverance

Remember the hurdles you crossed and the sacrifices you made. The late-night budgeting, the strict savings regimen, the sacrifices on wants for needs — all these actions display grit and perseverance. And these qualities inevitably bring success. Once you reach your goal – meeting the closing costs, securing the mortgage, and finally holding the keys to your new home – take a moment to reward your grit and perseverance.

13.5. Celebrating New Beginnings

Standing on the porch of your dream home, considering the journey you undertook, the challenges you faced, and the triumphs you enjoyed - this is a moment of celebration, a new beginning. It's the day you not only own a new house, but also the moment you reach long-desired financial autonomy.

In conclusion, the journey to financial autonomy is long and often winding. But as you set out on this path, keep your eyes fully open to the details - acknowledging and celebrating all your successes, no matter how seemingly minor they may be. Recognize this journey as an opportunity to witness your transformation towards financial freedom, cherishing and celebrating each victory along the way. Your final destination, the pleasure of homeownership and financial autonomy, is an enjoyable reward in itself but do not overlook the joy that comes from the journey itself.